Post-Communist Transition:
Some Lessons

Post-Communist Transition:
Some Lessons

Post-Communist Transition: Some Lessons

LESZEK BALCEROWICZ

THIRTY-FIRST WINCOTT LECTURE

8 OCTOBER 2001

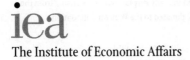

The Institute of Economic Affairs

First published in Great Britain in 2002 by
The Institute of Economic Affairs
2 Lord North Street
Westminster
London SW1P 3LB
in association with Profile Books Ltd

ISBN 0 255 36533 0

Many IEA publications are translated into languages other than English or
are reprinted. Permission to translate or to reprint should be sought from the
General Director at the address above.

The Trustees of the IEA have agreed that any surplus over costs arising from the
sale of this paper should be donated to the Wincott Foundation.

Typeset in Stone by MacGuru
info@macguru.org.uk

Printed and bound in Great Britain by Hobbs the Printers

CONTENTS

THE AUTHOR

Leszek Balcerowicz was born in Lipno, near Torun, Poland, in 1947. He graduated with distinction from the Faculty of Foreign Trade of the Central School of Planning and Statistics in Warsaw (now Warsaw School of Economics) in 1970. He received an MBA degree at St John's University in New York in 1974 and a doctor's degree in 1975. In September 1989 he became Deputy Prime Minister and Minister of Finance in the first non-communist government in Poland after World War II. He was also President of the Economic Committee of the Council of Ministers. He implemented a plan of rapid stabilisation and transformation of the Polish economy, widely known as the 'Balcerowicz plan'. He retained his positions in the government until December 1991. In 1992 he became a professor at the Warsaw School of Economics, and in 1993 head of the Chair of International Comparative Studies.

From 1997 to 2000 he was Deputy Prime Minister and Minister of Finance of the Republic of Poland and President of the Economic Committee of the Council of Ministers. In 2001 he was made President of the National Bank of Poland.

He is the author of over one hundred publications on economic affairs. He has lectured at many foreign universities, including in France, Great Britain, Japan and the United States. He has received ten honorary doctorates. In 1992 he received the prestigious Ludwig Erhard Award. In 1998 he received the 'Finance Minister of the

Year' title from the British financial monthly *Euromoney*. In 1999, the European Institute of Washington granted him the Transatlantic Leadership Award for the most outstanding European personality in 1998. In 1998, he received the Central European Award for the 1998 Finance Minister of the Year in Central and Eastern Europe. In 2000 he was awarded the Friedrich von Hayek Prize. In 2001, he received the Carl Bertelsmann Prize for his achievements during the process of transformation of the Polish economy. In 2002, the Fasel Foundation honoured him with a prize for his merits for the social market economy.

FOREWORD

A central theme in the journalistic work of Harold Wincott was the link between free markets, democracy and economic success. This has been reflected in many of the annual lectures that have been held in his memory since 1970. Past Wincott lecturers include such distinguished economists as Milton Friedman, F.A. Hayek, George Stigler, Jan Tumlir and Jagdish Bhagwati, all of whom have made important and original contributions to the study of how markets work.

Given this background, the trustees of the Wincott Foundation were delighted to welcome, as the 2001 Wincott Lecturer, Professor Leszek Balcerowicz, who has played a central role over the past decade in guiding Poland's transition from communism to democracy. As Deputy Prime Minister and Minister of Finance in the country's first post-war government, between 1989 and 1991, he was largely responsible for devising and implementing a reform programme which set Poland on the path towards a well-functioning market economy. He held the same posts between 1997 and 2000, and is currently President of the Polish central bank.

Professor Balcerowicz's experience in government, together with his close observation of how the same transition has been handled in other ex-communist countries, informs the analysis that was set out in his Wincott lecture, and is now published, in a slightly longer form, in this paper.

One of the key points to emerge from the paper is the importance of policy choices in determining how well or badly the various ex-communist countries managed the transition process. As Professor Balcerowicz points out, the starting point when the process began in the early 1990s varied widely from country to country. Some countries were exceptionally dependent for their exports on the former Soviet Union, and were hit hard by the collapse of the Soviet economy. Some were situated close to western Europe, and had a realistic prospect of becoming members of the European Union. Some had rich oil and gas reserves which, if used wisely, could support the reform programme. But none of these prior conditions mattered as much as the decisions taken by the early post-communist governments.

Professor Balcerowicz shows that, when looked at over a ten-year period, differences in growth performance are mostly due to the different extent of market-oriented reforms, especially economic liberalisation. 'The larger the scope of these reforms, the better, on average, the growth record.'

In discussing the political economy of transition, Professor Balcerowicz notes that in the immediate aftermath of the fall of communism there was a period of extraordinary political opportunity which some countries, including Poland, used to launch radical reforms. The subsequent extension of those reforms has had to take place in more normal political circumstances, and resistance from those who see themselves as losers from the reforms has become stronger. Even the most successful reforms produce discontent, and this poses a considerable challenge to political leaders. They have to convince their electorates that slowing down the pace of reform, while it may satisfy special-interest groups in the short term, will lead to a worse situation for the country as a whole.

All this is highly relevant, not just to policy-makers in the ex-communist countries, but also to the wider debate in Europe and the US about the future of global capitalism. As Professor David Henderson showed in his 2000 Wincott Lecture, *Anti-Liberalism 2000*, the general shift from statism to free markets which began in the 1980s and accelerated in the 1990s has generated a powerful backlash against what has been called 'the Washington consensus' – the belief that countries which open up their markets to free trade and free capital movements are likely to perform better than those which do not.

The anti-globalisation protesters, who have had some success in influencing government policy, notably in Europe, draw much of their inspiration from a false analysis of what free markets are doing to the world, suggesting, for example, that the activities of the World Trade Organisation are leading to increased inequality between and within nations, and worsening poverty in much of the developing world.

The best way to counter these misconceptions is by promoting a clearer understanding of what the transition to a market economy actually involves. Professor Balcerowicz's well-argued paper makes an immensely valuable contribution to this debate.

SIR GEOFFREY OWEN
Chairman of the Trustees
The Wincott Foundation
May 2002

ACKNOWLEDGEMENTS

I am very grateful to the Wincott Trustees for honouring me with the invitation to give the 2001 Wincott Lecture. I would especially like to thank the Chairman of the Trustees, Sir Geoffrey Owen. The text that follows constituted the basis for my lecture but goes beyond it, drawing upon the now substantial body of literature on the post-communist transition process. Given the limitations of space, the presentation of this enormous topic had to be very selective and focused on the most general and, I hope, fundamental issues.

I obtained helpful comments from my wife, Ewa Balcerowicz, on an earlier draft of this paper. I am also grateful to Remigusz Nawrat for his assistance in reviewing the empirical literature on economic transition in the post-communist countries, and to Malgorzata Kloc-Konkolowicz for her help in editing the text.

LESZEK BALCEROWICZ

July 2002

SUMMARY

- Post-communist transition in Europe and the former Soviet Union is one of the most important transformations in modern history. Like other radical shifts in history, its timing and its crucial events were totally unexpected.
- In the post-communist transition, compared with other transitions, changes were exceptionally large. Both political and economic systems were affected, there were changes in the social structure, territorial boundaries in some cases had to be established, and new institutions had to be constructed.
- It takes more time to privatise the bulk of a state-dominated economy than to arrange free elections and to create the rudiments of political parties.
- Market-oriented reforms had to be introduced under democratic (or at least pluralistic) political regimes in the post-communist transition. Most other transitions have had market reforms introduced by non-democratic regimes.
- The post-communist transition was also characterised by the absence of violence.
- Communist regimes tried to exert total control over individual activities and had overgrown welfare states. These regimes were therefore hugely overextended. Radical restructuring was needed in the transition – extension of liberties, reduction of taxes and the building of the

institutions of a free economy.

- Countries in the former Soviet bloc have achieved strikingly different economic outcomes since transformation began. Central and eastern European and the Baltic states did best between 1989 and 2000; the performance of ex-Soviet Union countries was much worse.

- Differences in initial conditions explain some of the variations in performance. But differences in policies are more important. The larger the scope of market-oriented reforms, the better the performance in terms of growth, low inflation and environmental improvement.

- State controls had blocked growth in former socialist economies. As they have been abolished, private entrepreneurship has been enabled and market institutions have been built.

- The presence of competent and determined reformers has been a crucial factor in successful transition. Individual reformers have seized opportunities and overcome resistance to change. Reform generates discontent – but in the long run non-radical reform produces more discontent.

TABLES

1   INTRODUCTION

'Transition' is usually meant to refer to a change in (or of) a country's institutional system, that is, a set of domestic institutions and the related mechanisms of individuals' interaction, such as the market (or central planning) or elections.

The institutional system includes, by definition, *inter alia*, the political and economic systems (for more on that see Balcerowicz, 1995). Therefore, one can distinguish 'political' and 'economic' transition (transformation). Both have a clear direction in most of the countries of Central and Eastern Europe (CEE) and the former USSR. Political transition refers to the changes in the role and structure of the state and to its democratisation. Economic transition denotes a movement from a socialist economy, a special case of a non-market system, towards a market economy with a growing share held by the private sector. Economic transition also includes, if necessary, macroeconomic stabilisation. If there is a large initial macroeconomic imbalance, such stabilisation requires, at least in the longer run, institutional (structural) reforms in the enterprise sector and in the fiscal sphere.

Post-communist transition in Europe and the former USSR was one of the most important transformations in modern history. Its timing and crucial events, especially during the early phase, were totally unexpected. No one had predicted that the Communist Party of the USSR would be disbanded by its General

Secretary, and that the Soviet Union would be peacefully dissolved by the presidents of Russia, Ukraine and Belarus. Other surprises included the unification of Germany and the disintegration of the former Czechoslovakia. All this confirms the general point that radical shifts in history are largely unpredictable.

On balance, the post-communist transition has been, I believe, a very positive process. One realises this when one compares the changes in welfare in countries differing from one another by the degree of reform. It is also important to remember that the no-transition scenario would not have meant maintaining the status quo of 1989 or 1991 but an inevitable gradual decay. Belarus under Lukashenko is probably the best factual example.

Popular disillusionment with reform should not be taken as a yardstick by which to judge post-communist transition, and certainly not as a reason to condemn it. As I am going to explain, even the most successful economic reforms inevitably produce considerable dissatisfaction, but little or no reform must sooner or later generate even greater disillusionment and frustration. It is also often the case that many people tend to blame 'reforms' for the social problems that result from their *absence*. Increased un-employment precipitated by labour market rigidity is a good case in point. Many intellectuals and ordinary people mentally ascribe anything and everything that has happened after the collapse of communism to 'transition'. Under such an erroneous definition the worst problems resulting from blocked reforms are blamed on reforms.

Post-communist transition is an enormous multi-dimensional topic. The present text has, obviously, to be very selective. Chapter 2 puts this transition into a comparative perspective. Chapter 3 provides a stylised description of the communist institutional

system. Chapter 4 focuses on the differences in economic performance among the post-communist countries and relates them to the
initial economic conditions and the extent of structural reforms.
Chapter 5 offers some observations on the political economy of
post-communist transition.

2 POST-COMMUNIST TRANSITION IN A COMPARATIVE PERSPECTIVE

The post-communist transition in CEE and the CIS has a number of important specific attributes, which become clear when we compare it with other major transformations.[1] They include 1) *classical transition*, meaning the extension of democracy in advanced capitalist countries between 1860 and 1920; 2) *neo-classical transition*, referring to democratisation in basically capitalist countries after World War II (West Germany, Italy and Japan in the 1940s; Spain and Portugal in the 1970s; some Latin American countries in the 1970s and 1980s; South Korea and Taiwan in the 1980s); 3) *market-oriented reform* in non-communist countries (West Germany and other Western countries after World War II; South Korea and Taiwan in the early 1960s; Chile in the 1970s; Turkey and Mexico in the 1980s; Argentina in the 1990s); and 4) Asian *post-communist transition* (China since the late 1970s and Vietnam since the late 1980s). There is, of course, much internal variety, especially within the first two categories. I will, however, disregard it here and focus on the fundamental differences *between*, rather than *within*, the respective types of transitions.

The post-communist transition in the former Soviet bloc was distinguished by a number of features, as shown in Table 1.

First, the scope of change was exceptionally large. Both po-

---

1   I am drawing here on Balcerowicz, 1995.

litical and economic systems were affected, and changes in these systems were compounded, in turn, by changes in the social structure. All these internal changes in the respective countries were brought about by, and took place within, the framework of the dissolution of the Soviet empire. Most of the post-Soviet countries faced the additional transition problems of defining their territorial as well as social and cultural boundaries, and of building their institutional apparatuses.

In most other cases of radical transition, there was either a focus on the political system while the economic system remained basically unchanged (as in classical and neo-classical transitions), or a focus on the economy while the political regime (usually non-democratic) was unaffected. The unprecedented scope of changes in the former Soviet bloc meant, among other things, an extreme information overload for decision-makers. Errors and delays were hardly surprising, especially since the decision-makers had to work with a public administration largely inherited from the old regime. A massive administrative turnover proved possible only in the former East Germany after reunification, an option obviously not open to other post-communist countries.

Second, although the changes in the political and economic systems *started* at about the same time, it is misleading to speak of simultaneous transition in post-communist Europe. It takes more time to privatise the bulk of a state-dominated economy than to organise free elections and to create at least some rudiments of political parties. Given the largely simultaneous beginnings of the political and economic transitions, this asymmetry in speed *produces a historically new sequence*: mass democracy (or at least political pluralism, that is, some degree of legal political competition) comes first and is followed by capitalism.

Table 1 Major transformations

	Classical	Neo-classical	Economic reforms in non-communist countries	Post-communist transition: China	Post-communist transition: former Soviet bloc
I. INITIAL CONDITIONS					
Political system					
In general	Restricted democracy	Authoritarian regimes	Varied: military dictatorship (Chile, Turkey); (West Germany, Japan); authoritarian regimes (S. Korea, Taiwan); quasi-authoritarian regime (Mexico); new democracy (Argentina under Menem)	Communist party-state	Communist party-state
Party system	Relatively developed	Suppressed	Suppressed	Suppressed	Suppressed
Economic system					
In general	Capitalist	Capitalist	'Suspended' capitalism (e.g. West Germany in 1948); or distorted capitalism (other countries)	Socialist, that is, 'destroyed' capitalism	Socialist, that is, 'destroyed' capitalism
Level of redistribution through the budget (social expenditure, welfare state)	Very low	Low or moderate	Rather low	Rather low	Very high
Socio-economic structure	Relatively industrialised	Varied: but most countries were relatively industrialised	Varied: from little industry to relatively industrialised	High share of easily privatisable agriculture	High share of socialist industry

II. FEATURES OF TRANSITION

Scope	Only political system	Only political system	Only or mostly economic system	Only economic system	Both political and economic system
Speed	Extension of suffrage gradual or in leaps	Rather rapid shift from non-democratic regime to mass democracy	Rather rapid stabilisation, liberalisation, often accompanied by privatisation	Rather rapid liberalisation and privatisation accompanied by periodic stabilisation of the overheated economy	Rapid shift from non-democratic to pluralist political arrangements, speed of economic reform varies
Sequence	First capitalism, then mass democracy	First capitalism, then mass democracy	First capitalism, then mass democracy	First capitalism, then mass democracy or at least political pluralism?	First mass democracy or at least political pluralism, then capitalism?
Extent of violence	Occasionally violent	Infrequently violent	Infrequently violent	Occasionally violent (Tiananmen Square)	Largely peaceful so far
Role of the mass media	Limited (no radio, no TV)	Important (radio, TV), a large increase in the role of mass media	Usually suppressed or controlled, except for economic reforms under new democracy (e.g. Argentina)	Suppressed	Large increase in the role of all mass media, especially radio and TV (visibility effect)
Role of external factors	Rather limited except for the cultural impact of the British model	Important: mass democracy became a dominant model of the political organisation (cultural diffusion)	Rather important: stable, liberal and outward-looking capitalist economy increasingly became a model in the 1970s and the 1980s	Limited; possibly authoritarian; 'Asian Tigers' as a model	Very important for countries besides the former USSR: without the collapse of the Soviet empire transition in those countries would have been impossible

Source: Balcerowicz, 1995.

Third, this sequence implies that it was necessary for market-oriented reforms, which had to be exceptionally comprehensive because of the socialist economic legacy, to be introduced under democratic, or at least pluralistic, political arrangements. Most other market-oriented reforms were introduced under non-democratic regimes (the third and fourth types of transition). Within this group, it is hard to find any case of economic transition that both approached the comprehensiveness of what occurred in post-communist Europe and was carried out under a democratic regime. Indeed, all the radical economic reforms elsewhere were introduced under clearly autocratic and rather oppressive regimes (Chile in the 1970s, China since the final years of that decade). There were some economic reforms carried out in democratic systems in the 1980s, including privatisation programmes in certain developed Western countries and stabilisation and structural adjustments in developing economies. Problems attributable to the democratic political environment did arise during these transitions, perhaps warning of similar hazards lurking in the much more comprehensive and complicated transitions of CEE.

These complications are, of course, far from being a sufficient argument for resorting to authoritarian solutions. This is so not only because of democracy's intrinsic importance to human dignity but also because authoritarian regimes do not inevitably promote rapid economic development (as they have done in South Korea and Taiwan). Many of them (such as Juan Perón's regime in Argentina or communist dictatorships) have disastrous effects on the economy.

A fourth exceptional feature of post-communist transition in CEE and the CIS is its relative lack of violence. True, some parts of the old communist-dominated East – in particular Yugoslavia, the Caucasus and areas of what used to be Soviet Central Asia – have seen terrible bloodshed. However, this was caused by the eruption of latent ethnic conflicts and/or the use of nationalism as an instrument for preserving dictatorial powers, but not by market-oriented reforms and democratisation. The countries of CEE have undergone a peaceful revolution, with massive changes in political and economic institutions initiated by negotiations between the outgoing communist elite and the leaders of the opposition. (The only case of violent transition in CEE took place in Romania, where no negotiations were held prior to the transfer of power.) Peaceful negotiations would never have taken place (or, had they taken place, they would never have borne fruit) had the Soviet threat not been gradually eliminated by Gorbachev's glasnost and perestroika. These negotiated changes were not always based on an explicit political pact and entailed a large element of surprise for all the main actors. However, they would not have come about if the members of the old elite had felt physically threatened or even if they had not believed that they would be free to seek favourable positions in whatever new system emerged. In this sense one can speak of tacit political pacts.

The non-violent nature of the transition in the former Soviet bloc, related to such political pacts, has had important implications for other aspects of the transitions. First, the old ruling elites have remained intact and stand ready to profit electorally from the dissatisfaction of a part of the population (which dissatisfaction, paradoxically, is likely to be greater than the economic desolation wrought by these old elites while in power). Second, the newly emerging capitalist class is likely to include some members of the former elites, a circumstance that tends to reduce the legitimacy of the whole capitalist transition and may fuel attacks by one sector of the former opposition against the sector currently in office. Such conflicts within the former opposition are good news for the forces of the old regime.

I have mentioned that a distinction is usually made between political and economic transition. There is, however, a large overlap between the two. On the one hand, some reforms that are usually labelled 'economic' are also a fundamental part of the political transformation. Privatisation of the economy determines its productivity growth, its supply response and the efficiency of the market mechanism. At the same time privatisation reduces the scope for political patronage, and constitutes, together with economic liberalisation, an indispensable condition for maintaining democracy.[2]

Economic liberalisation in a narrow sense – that is, eliminating the barriers to entry and supply, price and foreign exchange controls, etc. – releases market forces and increases productivity, but also reduces the dependence of individuals on the state. Many intellectuals who are for democracy but against radical market-oriented reforms neglect these important links.

On the other hand, some reforms usually called 'political' have both political and economic consequences. For example, the efficiency and fairness of the justice system are fundamentally important in terms of limiting the arbitrary power of the state as well as in the enforcement of property rights and contracts, and thus in longer-run economic development.

Given these caveats, I will first discuss the economic aspects

2   For more on this see Balcerowicz, 1995.

of transition, and then its socio-political dimensions. However, I shall begin with a brief description of the inherited communist institutional system, since the main directions of post-communist transition may be derived from the nature of the system.

3 THE COMMUNIST INSTITUTIONAL SYSTEM: A STYLISED DESCRIPTION

The nature of this system can be usefully reduced to the peculiarity of the communist party-state. It was a special case of dictatorship. Just as in other non-democratic regimes, where the succession of political rulers is based on mechanisms besides free elections, the communist system's leaders gained power by means of political struggle and bargaining within the elite of the single party.

The peculiarity of the communist party-state consisted in the attempt to have *total control over the individual's activities* – in other words, in the radical curtailment of individual liberties. This was especially true of economic freedoms, and especially striking when one compares the communist party-state with the autocratic regimes of East Asia, that is until their democratisation.

The controls exerted by the communist state were exceptionally extensive:

- private entrepreneurship was banned, which, together with the initial nationalisations, resulted in the monopoly of the state sector;[1]
- state-owned enterprises were subject to central planning,

---

1   In the former Yugoslavia this monopoly was granted to the labour-managed firms, which were subject to the Party nomenclature mechanisms but enjoyed more economic freedom than the state-owned enterprises (SOEs) under the Soviet system.

which included output commands, rationing of inputs and foreign exchange, price controls and directed foreign trade;

- the range of financial assets available to enterprises and individuals was extremely limited, as a market-type financial system could not have coexisted with central planning;
- the setting up and functioning of non-economic organisations were also heavily controlled; that is, civil society was suppressed and opposition political parties were banned;
- foreign travel was restricted;
- media were subject to formal censorship, direct party controls and personnel policy – mass media were largely an instrument of communist state propaganda;
- the juridical system was subordinated to the requirements of the command economy and to the suppression of individuals' political activity – political police played a prominent role.

These extensive controls coexisted with an *overgrown communist welfare state*. It included relatively large transfers in kind (education, health) and social protection delivered via state-owned enterprises (SOEs), artificially low prices for foodstuffs and energy and low housing rents. The social safety net, typical of some market economies, did not exist, as the need for it was sharply limited through the curtailment of individuals' opportunities and risks. The essence of the communist state consisted, therefore, in sharply limited individual liberties (especially economic ones) and extensive social entitlements.

In terms of the extensive controls and an overgrown welfare state one can clearly see that the communist state was hugely over-extended. One of its few positive legacies was a relatively high level of general education.

While the communist state was over-extended, it was also peculiar with respect to the *provision of public goods*. Defence expenditures were excessive and shaped by the imperial aspirations of the ruling elite of the Soviet Communist Party. In addition, at least from the point of view of the subordinated societies of the CEE and the Baltic states, the army was directed against the wrong enemy, that is, the West. Law and order were kept at a reasonable level, however, at the cost of practices typical of a police state. The legal framework and the juridical system criminalised private economic activity and independent political activity, and were ill suited to the market economy, rule of law and free society.

This brief description of the communist institutional system reveals that successful transition was tantamount to radical restructuring which, in turn, can be broken down into two main thrusts of structural reform:

1. Broadly defined liberalisation, that is, radical extension of civil, economic and political liberties by dismantling various controls, such as the ban on independent organisations, media censorship, central planning, etc. Reducing excessive tax burdens may also be included under liberalisation.
2. Building or restructuring institutions conducive to, or required by, free society and a stable and dynamic market economy.

Liberalisation enables private entrepreneurship, market forces and democratisation of the political system. Institution-building refers, first of all, to those parts of the state structures which provide public goods, such as protection of the extended individual rights (liberties), law and order and macroeconomic stability. It also includes the development of institutions that underpin the growth of the market-type financial system. The reform of the tax system, the restructuring of the inherited public administration, the establishment of a basic safety net, separate both from enterprises and the price system, are also important examples of institution-building.

Privatisation of SOEs, a fundamental economic reform with important political implications, can be included both under liberalisation and institution-building. It eliminates systematic and detailed state intervention and, as a result, creates institutions more conducive to a market economy and economic development.

4 INITIAL CONDITIONS, EXTENT OF REFORMS, ECONOMIC PERFORMANCE

A simple analytical framework

Any transition may be analysed by means of a simple analytical scheme which consists of four variables:

1. Initial (inherited) conditions.
2. Developments independent of the transition process but influencing its outcomes.
3. Behaviour of the relevant actors; in the case of countrywide transition this refers, first of all, to state policies.
4. Outcomes (performance).

Initial economic conditions include macroeconomic (im)balances, economic structure, stock of physical and human capital, size of the economy, its location, demographic structure, etc. They may be divided into lasting ones (such as location) and short-lived ones (most of the remaining conditions). In the context of market-oriented reforms, initial economic conditions may also be usefully divided into covert treasures and covert burdens (Balcerowicz, 1995). The word 'covert' refers to the fact that the impact of both was largely suppressed under central planning but would be enabled through economic liberalisation and the collapse of the Soviet trading system (Comecon).

Covert treasures are inherited conditions which, given the right policies, contribute to economic growth. The relevant examples include the large share of repressed but easily privatisable sectors,[1] a large pool of educated people or a favourable location – for example, bordering Western economies.

Hidden burdens are inherited conditions which, at least in the short run, negatively affect economic growth even under the right policies. Large trade dependence on the Soviet market, over-industrialisation or unfavourable location are the main examples.

Some of the inherited conditions may be termed mixed blessings, as they may turn into assets under the right policies and into liabilities under the wrong ones. In addition, they may influence the policies themselves (Sachs and Warner, 1995). The main examples of this category are mineral resources, especially oil and gas. Properly used, they would help to finance the development of infrastructure and the restructuring of other parts of the economy. Appropriated into private fortunes made early on, they could perform this function only to a limited extent. In addition, the newly created and spectacular inequalities would poison the social climate after the collapse of communism. Russia is obviously a case in point here.

Independent factors affecting the outcomes include, first of all, external economic developments. Their impact depends on the country's size and the related degree of openness. In the early phase after the collapse of communism these developments were largely determined by the inherited trade links, that is, the initial

---

1   Chinese agriculture in the late 1970s, at the start of economic reforms, is a prime example. Russia in the early 1990s had a much lower share of agriculture which, in addition, was not so easy to privatise.

conditions. With the passage of time these and other economic links change, depending on policies.

Initial conditions are determined by history, and external economic developments are shaped by forces independent of transition countries. Therefore *policies* are the only instruments by which a society may achieve good outcomes. The policies themselves depend on a web of interacting factors, analysed by political economics, including that branch dealing with reforms (for more on this see Balcerowicz, 1997). Domestic political developments crucially influence the direction and quality of policies. One can argue that these developments had their own dynamics in the transition countries, which were largely independent of the policies but, as pointed out, influenced them (Balcerowicz, 1995; EBRD, 2001). Therefore, not only external economic developments but also domestic political developments enter the category of independent factors influencing the outcomes.

Finally, *outcomes* refer to changes – over an analysed period – in those variables which represent society's welfare. A typical measure of economic transition is GDP growth after the collapse of communism. Other measures may include productivity growth, foreign direct investment (FDI) inflows, inflation, health and environmental indicators.

The basic analytical task is to explain the differences in the outcomes by linking them to the differences in policies and in other factors (in the inherited conditions and in the partly related external economic developments).

Different economic outcomes

The striking fact about the countries in the former Soviet bloc is that they achieved hugely different economic outcomes only a couple of years after the collapse of communism. In other words, the differences in the standard of living among them are now much larger than those in a not very distant past:

The official data show that the real GDP in 2000 equalled 107 per cent of that in 1989 in CEE and the Baltic states while the comparable figure for the CIS was 61 per cent (EBRD, 2001).

The figures for individual countries also vary much more:[2]

Poland	127
Slovenia	114
Hungary	104
Slovakia	103
Czech Republic	98
Estonia	83
Romania	77
Bulgaria	71
Kirghizia	66
Lithuania	65
Latvia	64
Russia	63
Armenia	63
Ukraine	42
Moldova	33

2 I am excluding countries that suffered GDP declines due to civil wars (Georgia, Tajikistan) and countries where statistical data are highly suspect because of their dictatorial political regimes (Belarus, Uzbekistan).

Anders Åslund (2001) thoroughly discusses the pitfalls of official statistics. He points out that the levels of GDP under communism were largely inflated due to wasteful investment, excessive stocks, large military expenditures and value-diminishing activities which were counted as positive contributions to GDP. As a result the true dynamics of real output after the collapse of communism were much more favourable than the official figures would indicate. Another reason was the growth of the unofficial economy, which, in addition, differed across transition countries. Åslund also stresses that a transition from the Soviet trading system to a market-based one involved the elimination of artificially low prices for oil and gas charged by Russia to other countries of the former Soviet bloc. Therefore, a substantial part of the recorded GDP decline in the importing countries was due to the elimination of these subsidies. They suffered a huge trade shock, the price for political independence. Correspondingly, the actual decline in Russia's GDP was smaller than the recorded one. However, these sensible corrections do not change the *relative* picture given by the official data. They would rather strengthen the relative GDP performance of small oil- and gas-importing counties such as the Baltics, Kirghizia or Armenia.

FDI inflows may also be regarded as an indicator of economic performance as they usually follow economic success (and strengthen the subsequent economic growth). The countries of the former Soviet bloc have achieved very different outcomes in this respect. The cumulative FDI inflows per capita (EBRD, 2001) were as follows:

	$US
Czech Republic	2102
Hungary	1964
Estonia	1400
Latvia	1056
Slovak Republic	772
Slovenia	756
Poland	751
Lithuania	646
Bulgaria	404
Romania	301
Armenia	145
Moldova	102
Kirghizia	93
Russia	69
Ukraine	68

The largest cumulative inflows of FDI, between 1989 and 2000, were attracted by Poland ($29 billion), followed by the Czech Republic ($21.7 billion), Hungary ($19.7 billion). Russia gained $10 billion, Romania $6.7 billion, Ukraine and Bulgaria had $3.3 billion each. With an economy of a similar initial size Poland has attracted nine times more FDI than Ukraine.

Countries which scored well on economic growth also achieved a high rate of productivity growth in industry. For the years 1996-2000, the figure for Poland is 53 per cent, for the Czech Republic 38.9 per cent, for Lithuania 31.8 per cent, for the Slovak Republic 28.3 per cent, and for Hungary 24.1 per cent (EBRD, 2001). No data are available for other transition economies but there is little doubt that the economic laggards must have also performed poorly in terms of productivity.

Transition countries have had a varying disinflation record. Generally speaking, better growth performance goes hand in hand with more macroeconomic stabilisation. The median inflation in CEE and the Baltics in 2000 was 5.7 per cent while the price level in Romania increased by 45.7 per cent, in Russia by 32.9 per cent, in Moldova by 31.3 per cent, and in Ukraine by 28.2 per cent (EBRD, 2001). This confirms a general point that in countries which inherited high inflation successful disinflation is conducive to longer-term economic growth.

Being highly wasteful, the Soviet-type economy was also very damaging to the environment. One of the main reasons for this was a high ratio of energy consumption to GDP (energy intensity). The transition countries have differed in the evolution of this measure, that is, in the impact of the economy on the environment. Energy intensity in CEE and the Baltics was reduced by 21 per cent between 1992 and 1998 while it increased by 5 per cent in the CIS (EBRD, 2001). On average, better growth performers have turned out to be also more environment-friendly than those lagging in economic growth.

The post-communist countries have displayed differing developments in public health. Life expectancy has increased in CEE while it has declined in Russia and Ukraine and stagnated in Bulgaria and Romania. Similar divergences can be detected with respect to child mortality (EBRD, 2001). Better growth performance has, therefore, been accompanied by more favourable health developments.

While optimal distribution of earnings cannot be established in an inter-subjective way, a sharply increased earning inequality (or a high level of inequality) is often regarded as a negative phenomenon. It is, therefore, interesting to compare the development of earnings inequality, as measured by the GINI coefficient, across those transition countries for which data are available (EBRD, 2001):

Bulgaria	26.2 (1991)	–	29.1 (1996)
Czech Republic	21.2 (1991)	–	25.9 (1997)
Hungary	30.5 (1992)	–	34.8 (1997)
Latvia	24.7 (1991)	–	33.6 (1997)
Lithuania	37.2 (1992)	–	34.5 (1997)
Poland	23.9 (1991)	–	30.0 (1997)
Romania	20.4 (1991)	–	42.2 (1997)
Russia	32.5 (1991)	–	48.3 (1996)
Slovenia	27.3 (1991)	–	30.7 (1997)
Ukraine	25.1 (1991)	–	41.3 (1996)

As one can see, the fastest increases and the highest levels of earnings inequality have been recorded by Russia, Romania and Ukraine, countries with a rather poor relative growth record. At the same time better growth performers (the Czech Republic, Hungary, Poland, Slovenia) have, on average, displayed lower growth and lower levels of GINI coefficient.

Explaining differences in outcomes

The enormous differentiation in outcomes in the post-communist countries, described above, obviously poses questions about its causes. Substantial literature dealing with this issue has already been compiled. It focuses on explaining the relative growth performance of these economies; much less attention has been paid to the determinants of the differences in other dimensions of welfare. It can be shown, however, that some crucial factors conducive to longer-run economic growth are also conducive to ecological improvement and to favourable health developments. In addition, these two variables are correlated to some extent. For countries that inherited a wasteful communist economy, increased economic efficiency, especially in the production and consumption of energy and raw materials, has been one of the fundamental factors in economic growth, which has had obvious ecological implications, too. Therefore, the differences in the evolution of this efficiency must have differentiated both growth and ecological performance. Different health developments can be linked to economic forces (for example, economic liberalisation changed the availability and relative prices of more and less (un)healthy foodstuffs), which also affect growth (Balcerowicz, 1998). Finally, differences in the ease of entry of new firms affect both economic growth and income inequality.

Turning to the differences in the growth performance of the post-communist economies, we must return to the question of what has been the relative role of the inherited economic conditions (and partly related external developments) and that of different policies.

The initial conditions were, on average, very difficult but at the same time highly varied (for more on this see World Bank, 2002). Countries differed very much with respect to the inherited hidden treasures and hidden burdens affecting future economic growth.

The small former Soviet republics heavily dependent on exports to Russia (such as the Baltics, Kirghizia, Georgia, Moldova, Armenia) were to suffer huge external shocks as a result of the collapse of the former Soviet Union and the Soviet trading system. And some of them were constrained in the reorientation of their foreign trade owing to their geographical distance from the West (for example, Kirghizia). They were bound to suffer the deepest initial decline in GDP. Being less dependent on the Soviet trading system, the CEE countries were exposed to less serious shocks to GDP. Russia was in the most favourable situation because its size meant that it was the least dependent on exports to other socialist economies. And as a large exporter of oil and gas to its former satellites, it was to obtain large terms-of-trade gains thanks to the collapse of Comecon and the switch to world prices of these minerals. Therefore, Russia's profound decline in official GDP between 1992 and 1996 cannot be explained by unfavourable external developments.

Other large differences in the initial economic conditions included the relative importance of heavy industry and mining, the magnitude of macroeconomic imbalances, and the level of foreign debt.

It appears that the best initial conditions – that is, those that produced relatively more economic gain and less economic pain – existed in the Czech Republic, which had a relatively good economic structure, a very favourable location, the most stable macroeconomic situation, and little foreign debt. The other extreme included, as mentioned, the smaller countries of the former Soviet Union which inherited very unstable economies and heavy structural dependence on the Soviet market. Examples of the intermediate category include Bulgaria (with the highest degree of dependence on the Soviet market in CEE), Poland (with hyperinflation, a large and inefficient coal-mining sector and a large foreign debt), and Romania (with an economy heavily distorted by years of Ceausescu's policies).

However large the differences in the initial economic conditions, they can explain only a part of the relative growth performance of the transition countries, and only in the early phase after the collapse of communism. The differences in longer-term growth performance are mostly due to different policies, that is, the different extent of market-oriented reforms, especially economic liberalisation. The larger the scope of these reforms, the better, on average, the growth record. These are the main conclusions of the empirical literature on transition economies. There is no single empirical study I know which shows that less reform was, under comparable conditions, better for economic growth than more reform.

Table 2 summarises the main findings of the three most recent studies on the determinants of growth in transition countries.

The extent of market-oriented reforms is measured in statistical studies by the liberalisation index developed by de Melo, Denizer and Gelb (1996) and by transition indicators of the European Bank for Reconstruction and Development. These measures capture first of all the economic aspects of liberalisation reforms, as described in Chapter 3. The strong statistical link between them and growth performance underlines how various state controls have blocked the growth of former socialist economies and how important it is to abolish them, thus enabling private entrepreneurship and market forces. These measures focus to a lesser extent on institution-building, the second category of post-socialist reforms, mentioned in Chapter 3.

However, a more casual analysis of the respective transition countries suggests that, on average, countries that have achieved a larger extent of liberalisation have also made larger advances in institution-building (and in macroeconomic stabilisation, which is

Table 2 **Extent of reforms and the growth performance in transition countries**

Authors	Sample	Results
Berg, Andrew, Borensztein, Eduardo, Sahay, Ratna, Zettelmeyer, Jeromin, 1999	26 countries in transition (10 CEE 1991–6)	• 'The "U" shape in output is explained by the combination of (i) post-communist initial conditions that, by themselves, generate a contraction in output, and (ii) structural reforms, which are the driving force of recovery.' • 'Even though structural reforms often affect private and state sectors in opposite ways, the net effect of structural reforms appears to be positive from the beginning, that is, we find little evidence that reforms significantly exacerbate the output decline initially.' • 'The impact of macroeconomic variables, although significant, is much smaller than that of either initial conditions or structural reforms.' • 'The role of initial conditions in explaining cross-sectional variation in growth is surprisingly minor; in particular, the difference in performance between the CEE and the BRO countries [the Baltics, Russia and other countries of the former Soviet Union] is mostly explained by differences in structural reforms (even at the beginning of transition), rather than initial conditions.' (p. 9)
Fischer, Stanley, Sahay, Ratna, 2000	25 transition countries 1989–98	• 'All three results [of three regressions by Fischer and Sahay] confirm that anti-inflation policies and structural reform policies were beneficial to growth.' • 'The experience accumulated in the past decade, whether viewed informally or with the help of data, charts, and regressions, provides support for the view that the most successful transition economies are those that have both stabilised and undertaken comprehensive reforms, and that more and faster reform is better than less and slower reform.' (p. 17)
Havrylyshyn, Oleh, Wolf, Thomas, 2001	25 transition countries up to 1997	• 'Unfavourable initial conditions should not become an excuse for inaction. Initial conditions such as heavier industrialization or a relative dearth of historical contacts with market economies can hamper recovery, but they are not insurmountable obstacles, for several reasons. First, their negative effects decline over time. Second, the empirical studies clearly suggest that these effects can be compensated by modestly faster progress on reforms. And third, perhaps the main fact is indirect; that is, unfavourable initial conditions result in less political will and capacity for reform, and less reform means less growth.' (p. 115)

linked both to liberalisation and institution-building). Therefore, we may conclude that the larger the extent of structural reforms leading away from the communist institutional system towards a rationally limited state and market economy, the better the growth performance. In other words, more transition produced more economic growth and, more generally, better economic performance.

5   ON THE POLITICAL ECONOMY OF TRANSITION

The purpose of this chapter is to focus on some selected issues relating to the political economy of transition. In this way we can gain, I hope, some insights into the determinants of the extent of structural reforms, which largely explain the differences in the economic performance of the post-communist economies (Chapter 4). Given the limitations of space, the analysis is far from complete.

The political breakthrough

The post-communist political transition had special dynamics – it started with a political breakthrough, which opened the way to a brief period of 'extraordinary politics', which in turn gave way to 'normal' partisan politics or, in some countries (for example, Uzbekistan, Belarus) to a renewed dictatorship. The first period was characterised by two transitional factors: post-liberalisation euphoria and special conditions in the political sphere (political forces of the former regime were still discredited and the opposition was still united). As a result, it was early in this period that difficult economic measures could be more readily accepted in the political system and in society at large (Balcerowicz, 1995).

The timing and intensity of the political breakthrough varied across countries. Earlier breakthroughs (Poland in the first half of 1989) in combination with a rapidly declining threat of Soviet intervention (the Gorbachev factor) contributed to later break-throughs in CEE, creating a sort of chain reaction. With respect to the former Soviet Union, the decisive event was the failed putsch in August 1991, which triggered the dissolution of the Soviet Union and the political and economic transitions in the former Soviet re-publics. As these started about two years after similar processes in CEE, they were able to profit from the experience of these earlier transitions.

The post-socialist countries also differed in nature and, as a result, in the psychological consequences of the political break-through. One can distinguish between Russia and the former So-viet republics on the one hand, with the least developed national awareness, and the remaining countries on the other. The external liberation of the societies of the second group must have been per-ceived by many Russians as a loss of both prestige and a sense of history. The newly gained independence must have meant much less to the countries with the least developed national aspirations than to the countries of CEE and to people in the Baltic states.

Differences in the depth of the political breakthrough imply that the countries also differed with respect to the length and intensity of 'extraordinary' politics and with regard to the related political climate for radical economic reform existing in the first phase. But the first period after the political breakthrough had in each country some special characteristics conducive to radical economic reform. The quick launching of such a reform may, therefore, be regarded as a proper use of the scarce 'political' capital given by history, while a delay would be a waste of these opportunities. But only some countries used the period of extra-ordinary politics to launch radical reforms; Poland was a pioneer in this respect. It appears that such reforms happened only in those countries where the new political forces assumed political power and where, in addition, the reform was carried out by a reform-minded economic team with a clear leader.

However, the period of 'extraordinary' politics was obviously too short for the completion of some fundamental reforms – privatisation, development of a mature financial system or pension reform. Therefore, even those countries which used the first period to launch radical reforms are facing the challenge of completing them in the later stages of 'normal' politics. But, most likely, the challenges would have been even greater had they not used the period of extraordinary politics to introduce radical reforms.

Democratisation empowered voters in the post-communist countries, and voters cannot choose between individual positions on various issues (individual 'commodities'), but rather have a choice only between 'bundles' of positions 'packaged' by the parties. This has probably had important implications for the chances of, and obstacles to, radical economic reforms. Support for such reforms can be linked to a popular position on another issue (that is, EU accession as against preserving national independence). This may be called a positive linkage. On the other hand, opposition to such reforms may still be linked to a popular position on another issue (for example, criticism of the loss of empire in Russian politics). We can then speak of a negative linkage.

The possibilities for creating such positive and negative linkages differed across post-communist countries, and these differences appear to have been related to the extent of market-oriented reforms. More radical reformers balanced these linkages better than less radical reformers. In the case of CEE and the Baltics, the prospect of EU accession constituted an important positive force for reforms. And voters in these countries, especially in the small Baltic states, characterised by high national awareness, could support radical economic programmes proposed by pro-independence forces because they trusted them and believed that such programmes were necessary to strengthen the economy and thus their newly gained independence.

Such positive linkages were not established by less radical reformers. The prospect of EU access was not available to them, and the strength of national awareness was on average less than among radical reformers (compare the Baltics and Belarus). Russia presents a special case. The collapse of the former Soviet Union was likely to produce not post-independence euphoria, as in its former satellites, but rather, as mentioned, disillusionment, disorientation and frustration. And it was possible for the communist opponents of radical economic reforms to mobilise these negative feelings.

The role of reformers

However, situational factors such as different inherited conditions and different combinations of positive and negative linkages cannot fully explain the differences in the extent of market-oriented reforms and the related differences in economic performance. Anybody acquainted with the history of post-communist reforms must notice the important role played by competent and determined reformers in the government, whose presence or absence is largely a chance factor. The personality factor does matter in history. The opportunities for radical reforms offered by relatively favourable situational factors could be missed without such individuals, while resistance to such reforms, a product of unfavourable situational factors, can be, at least partially, overcome if such persons happen to be in a position of power. The first case can be illustrated, I believe, by the early years of Hungarian economic reform, and the second by the radical reforms in Kirghizia, where a reformist president, Akayev, has made them his strategic priority.

Liberalisation and the mass media

Political liberalisation has freed the mass media. The controlled media of the communist era did not engage in any regular presentation and criticism of the reality of communism. Politically controlled, they displayed a 'positive bias'. In contrast, the newly freed mass media tended to focus on the negative aspects of the new, post-communist reality, as bad news usually attracts more attention than good news. Therefore, they displayed a 'negative bias' in presenting post-communist developments. This shift from a positive to a negative bias, largely a natural by-product of political liberalisation and the modus operandi of free media, must have had an important impact on the political opinions and choices of the newly empowered voters. It must have blackened their perception of the newly emerging reality compared to that of its communist predecessor. The inherited statistical systems, which were unable to cope with the new economic reality and underestimated the effects and overestimated the costs of economic reforms, were one of the sources of the negative views of the post-communist reality.[1] As a result, a 'regime shift' in mass media, an important and beneficial component of

---

[1]   For example, in Poland the final figures that put the decline in GDP, 1990–1, at 5–10 per cent as compared to the original 18–20 per cent were not published at all, while the latter were given a lot of publicity.

the whole post-communist transformation in itself, paradoxically strengthened nostalgia for communism and reinforced the political position of anti-reformist and post-communist forces (these two often overlapped).

However, the strength of the negative bias in the presentation of the post-communist reality may have differed among the transition countries, depending on the quality of journalists, and especially their ability to distinguish between the effects of the inherited conditions and those of reforms. These differences may then have contributed to the differences in the extent of reforms through their impact on electoral results.

Reform and discontent

Given the challenging initial conditions and unfavourable external developments (especially the collapse of trade within Comecon) that faced each country in CEE during the post-communist transition, each type of economic policy was bound to generate discontent in some sections of the populace. In addition to turning disguised unemployment into open unemployment, radical economic reform also increased discontent simply by broadening the scope of general economic freedom. Since only some people can directly take advantage of the new opportunities, others may feel resentment, especially if they view the new winners as undeserving. Rapid shifts occur in the relative pay and prestige of various occupations and professional groups as markets replace the planned socialist economy. Miners, heavy-industrial workers and other groups that see themselves as 'losers' – even if only in relative terms – are likely to be dissatisfied. There is, moreover, an unavoidable trade-off between opportunity and security. This hard truth may be poorly understood and bitterly disliked, especially by those who experience a much larger increase in insecurity than in perceived opportunities.

However, given the same difficult initial and external conditions, slow or no reform will also produce discontent, though in different ways. If the initial macroeconomic situation is highly unstable, non-radical economic reform will find itself immediately bedevilled by high and growing inflation, which produces its own version of severe economic insecurity. Non-radical reform programmes do this by preferring covert to overt unemployment. Covert unemployment is less psychologically painful to the persons concerned, but it must be financed through fiscal or quasi-fiscal subsidies, which in turn spur inflation. The result is inflation-bred insecurity and dissatisfaction. Moreover, it must be kept in mind that any future attempts at macroeconomic stabilisation will flush covert unemployment out into the open.

Non-radical programmes, which typically feature less liberalisation and correspondingly more state intervention, also give rise to new economic inequalities, with the 'winners' being those who can successfully lobby government. In practice, this means members of the old communist elite, who are more experienced, better organised and better connected than others. The inequalities generated by their lobbying are less justified by economic performance than those that stem from radical reform programmes and rankle with the 'losers' even more. Finally, by channelling entrepreneurial and managerial energies into rent-seeking and corruption rather than into the search for greater efficiency, non-radical programmes that avoid liberalisation destroy the prospects for economic development. Anyone willing to take the longer view should then realise that the discontent and drawbacks associated with non-radical reform outweigh the problems brought by sustained and radical efforts towards comprehensive liberalisation, stabilisation and institutional building.

6 CONCLUDING REMARKS

Countries which inherited the communist institutional system had to launch and implement two basic kinds of structural reforms: exceptionally comprehensive liberalisation and the vast programme of building or restructuring of institutions conducive to, or required by, free society and a stable and dynamic market economy. These post-communist reforms have been an especially spectacular case of a broader tendency to reduce the excesses of statism and to move to free markets, present in Western countries and in many developing ones.

The experience of post-communist countries strongly suggests that more extensive structural reforms produce better growth performance as well as lower inflation, more favourable ecological and health developments, and less growth in earnings inequality.

Even the most successful reforms inevitably produce considerable discontent. However, slow reforms, or no reforms at all, are bound to produce even greater dissatisfaction.

REFERENCES

Åslund, Anders (2001), *Building Capitalism. The Transformation of the Former Soviet Bloc*, Cambridge University Press, Cambridge.

Balcerowicz, Leszek (1995), *Socialism, Capitalism, Transformation*, Central European University Press, Budapest.

Balcerowicz, Leszek (1997), 'The Interplay between Economic and Political Transition', in Salvatore Zecchini (ed.), *Lessons from the Economic Transition. Central and Eastern Europe in the 1990's*, Kluwer Academic Publishers, Norwell, Mass.

Balcerowicz, Leszek (1998), 'Economic Forces and Health', in *Dialogue and Universalism*, 8.

Berg, Andrew, Eduardo Borensztein, Ratna Sahay, and Jeromin Zettelmayer (1999), *The Evolution of Output in Transition Economies: Explaining the Differences*, IMF Working Paper No. 73, Washington, DC.

De Melo, Martha, Eduardo Denizer, and Alan Gelb (1996), 'From Plan to Market: Pattern of Transition', in *World Bank Economic Review*, 15 (1).

EBRD (European Bank for Reconstruction and Development) (2001), *Transition Report 2001*, London.

Fischer, Stanley, and Ratna Sahay (2000), *Transition Economies after Ten Years*, IMF Working Paper No. 30, Washington, DC.

Havrylyshyn, Oleh, and Thomas Wolf (2001), 'Growth in
      Transition Countries, 1990–1998: The Main Lessons', in O.
      Havrylyshyn and S. Nsouli (eds), *A Decade of Transition:
      Achievements and Challenges*, IMF.
Sachs, Jeffrey, and Andrew Warner (1995), 'Economic Growth
      and the Process of Global Integration', in *Brookings Papers on
      Economic Activity*.
World Bank (2002), *Transition: The First Ten Years. Analysis
      and Lessons for Eastern Europe and the Former Soviet Union*,
      Washington, DC.

ABOUT THE IEA

The Institute is a research and educational charity (No. CC 235 351), limited by guarantee. Its mission is to improve understanding of the fundamental institutions of a free society with particular reference to the role of markets in solving economic and social problems.

The IEA achieves its mission by:

- a high-quality publishing programme
- conferences, seminars, lectures and other events
- outreach to school and college students
- brokering media introductions and appearances

The IEA, which was established in 1955 by the late Sir Antony Fisher, is an educational charity, not a political organisation. It is independent of any political party or group and does not carry on activities intended to affect support for any political party or candidate in any election or referendum, or at any other time. It is financed by sales of publications, conference fees and voluntary donations.

In addition to its main series of publications the IEA also publishes a quarterly journal, *Economic Affairs*, and has two specialist programmes – Environment and Technology, and Education.

The IEA is aided in its work by a distinguished international Academic Advisory Council and an eminent panel of Honorary Fellows. Together with other academics, they review prospective IEA publications, their comments being passed on anonymously to authors. All IEA papers are therefore subject to the same rigorous independent refereeing process as used by leading academic journals.

IEA publications enjoy widespread classroom use and course adoptions in schools and universities. They are also sold throughout the world and often translated/reprinted.

Since 1974 the IEA has helped to create a world-wide network of 100 similar institutions in over 70 countries. They are all independent but share the IEA's mission.

Views expressed in the IEA's publications are those of the authors, not those of the Institute (which has no corporate view), its Managing Trustees, Academic Advisory Council members or senior staff.

Members of the Institute's Academic Advisory Council, Honorary Fellows, Trustees and Staff are listed on the following page.

The Institute gratefully acknowledges financial support for its publications programme and other work from a generous benefaction by the late Alec and Beryl Warren.

57

THE WINCOTT MEMORIAL LECTURES

Other papers recently published by the IEA include:

WHO, What and Why?

Transnational Government, Legitimacy and the World Health Organization
Roger Scruton
Occasional Paper 113; ISBN 0 255 36487 3
£8.00

The World Turned Rightside Up

A New Trading Agenda for the Age of Globalisation
John C. Hulsman
Occasional Paper 114; ISBN 0 255 36495 4
£8.00

The Representation of Business in English Literature

Introduced and edited by Arthur Pollard
Readings 53; ISBN 0 255 36491 1
£12.00

Anti-Liberalism 2000

The Rise of New Millennium Collectivism
David Henderson
Occasional Paper 115; ISBN 0 255 36497 0
£7.50

Capitalism, Morality and Markets
Brian Griffiths, Robert A. Sirico, Norman Barry & Frank Field
Readings 54; ISBN 0 255 36496 2
£7.50

A Conversation with Harris and Seldon
Ralph Harris & Arthur Seldon
Occasional Paper 116; ISBN 0 255 36498 9
£7.50

Malaria and the DDT Story
Richard Tren & Roger Bate
Occasional Paper 117; ISBN 0 255 36499 7
£10.00

A Plea to Economists Who Favour Liberty: Assist the Everyman
Daniel B. Klein
Occasional Paper 118; ISBN 0 255 36501 2
£10.00

Waging the War of Ideas
John Blundell
Occasional Paper 119; ISBN 0 255 36500 4
£10.00

The Changing Fortunes of Economic Liberalism

Yesterday, Today and Tomorrow
David Henderson
Occasional Paper 105 (new edition); ISBN 0 255 36520 9
£12.50

The Global Education Industry

Lessons from Private Education in Developing Countries
James Tooley
Hobart Paper 141 (new edition); ISBN 0 255 36503 9
£12.50

Saving Our Streams

*The Role of the Anglers' Conservation Association in
Protecting English and Welsh Rivers*
Roger Bate
Research Monograph 53; ISBN 0 255 36494 6
£10.00

Better Off Out?

The Benefits or Costs of EU Membership
Brian Hindley & Martin Howe
Occasional Paper 99 (new edition); ISBN 0 255 36502 0
£10.00

Buckingham at 25
Freeing the Universities from State Control
Edited by James Tooley
Readings 55; ISBN 0 255 36512 8
£15.00

Lectures on Regulatory and Competition Policy
Irwin M. Stelzer
Occasional Paper 120; ISBN 0 255 36511 X
£12.50

Misguided Virtue
False Notions of Corporate Social Responsibility
David Henderson
Hobart Paper 142; ISBN 0 255 36510 1
£12.50

HIV and Aids in Schools
The Political Economy of Pressure Groups and Miseducation
Barrie Craven, Pauline Dixon, Gordon Stewart & James Tooley
Occasional Paper 121; ISBN 0 255 36522 5
£10.00

The Road to Serfdom

The Reader's Digest *condensed version*
Friedrich A. Hayek
Occasional Paper 122; ISBN 0 255 36530 6
£7.50

Bastiat's *The Law*

Introduction by Norman Barry
Occasional Paper 123; ISBN 0 255 36509 8
£7.50

A Globalist Manifesto for Public Policy

Charles Calomiris
Occasional Paper 124; ISBN 0 255 36525 X
£7.50

Euthanasia for Death Duties

Putting Inheritance Tax Out of Its Misery
Barry Bracewell-Milnes
Research Monograph 54; ISBN 0 255 36513 6
£10.00

Liberating the Land
The Case for Private Land-use Planning
Mark Pennington
Hobart Paper 143; ISBN 0 255 36508 X
£10.00

IEA Yearbook of Government Performance 2002/ 2003
Edited by Peter Warburton
Yearbook 1; ISBN 0 255 36532 2
£15.00

Britain's Relative Economic Performance, 1870– 1999
Nicholas Crafts
Research Monograph 55; ISBN 0 255 36524 1
£10.00

Should We Have Faith in Central Banks?
Otmar Issing
Occasional Paper 125; ISBN 0 255 36528 4
£7.50

The Dilemma of Democracy

Arthur Seldon

Hobart Paper 136 (reissue); ISBN 0 255 36536 5

£10.00

Capital Controls: a 'Cure' Worse Than the Problem?

Forrest Capie

Research Monograph 56; ISBN 0 255 36506 3

£10.00

The Poverty of 'Development Economics'

Deepak Lal

Hobart Paper 144 (reissue); ISBN 0 255 36519 5

£15.00

Should Britain Join the Euro?

The Chancellor's Five Texts Examined

Patrick Minford

Occasional Paper 126; ISBN 0 255 36527 6

£7.50

To order copies of currently available IEA papers, or to enquire about availability, please write (no postage required from within the UK) to:

Lavis Marketing
IEA orders
FREEPOST LON21280
Oxford OX3 7BR

Or contact Lavis Marketing on:
Tel: 01865 767575
Fax: 01865 750079
Email: orders@lavismarketing.co.uk

The IEA also offers a subscription service to its publications. For a single annual payment, currently £40.00 in the UK, you will receive every title the IEA publishes across the course of a year, invitations to events, and discounts on our extensive back catalogue. For more information, please contact:

Subscriptions
The Institute of Economic Affairs
2 Lord North Street
London SW1P 3LB

Tel: 020 7799 8900
Fax: 020 7799 2137
Website: www.iea.org.uk